SIGN OF CONTRADICTION: THE CHRISTMAS STORY

STEPHEN CALLAGHAN

First Edition. 2020.
Independently Published.
ISBN: 9798562022493

Sign of Contradiction: The Christmas Story
© Stephen Callaghan 2018

**Permission to publicly perform this play, in part or
in whole, by any person or organisation, amateur or
professional must be sought in advance from the
author.**

**To obtain a licence to publicly perform this play,
please visit: www.stephencallaghan.com**

Stephen Callaghan is a prolific playwright and theatre-maker, based in Glasgow, Scotland. He has written extensively on faith-related subjects, from the lives of Saints to Biblical material in new and challenging ways. Often infused with the humour and style of his native city, his plays have been performed widely in local venues and schools around Scotland and at the Edinburgh Fringe Festival. These include a commission from the Vatican for an International Conference taking place in Glasgow in 2020 and the acclaimed "The Margaret Sinclair Story", commissioned by the Archdiocese of St Andrews and Edinburgh, which premiered at the Edinburgh Fringe in 2016. Together with his wife, Rachel, he directs the work of Callaghan Theatre Productions and is also the Creative Director of the Archdiocese of Glasgow Arts Project (AGAP). He is a member of the Scottish Society of Playwrights, an Honours graduate of the University of Glasgow Theatre, Film & TV Studies Department and holds Licentiate and Associate diplomas in Speech and Drama from the London College of Music and Media.

www.stephencallaghan.com

Other Plays by Stephen Callaghan

Sign of Contradiction: The Passion Story
Sign of Contradiction: The Christmas Story
The Pew With a View
The Margaret Sinclair Story
Passionate Voices
Feet of Clay
Paul
The Curé D'Ars: A Priest Forever
Pure Dead Dangerous
The Turnaround
The Martyrdom of Saint John Ogilvie
The Pilgrimage
The Stations of the Cross
A Wean in A Manger
Among Women
Father Kentenich: Champion of Freedom
Mungo: The Legend of Glasgow's Saint
Wilderness

SIGN OF CONTRADICTION: THE CHRISTMAS STORY

A Play recounting the events surrounding the Nativity of Jesus Christ.

"Sign of Contradiction: A Different Kind of Nativity Play"

By Stephen Callaghan

Think of the word "Nativity" and you probably think of small children wearing tea towels on their heads. It is a story that is part of our childhood and has at its heart one particular Child who changed the course of human history. When I wrote Sign of Contradiction: The Christmas Story, I was awaiting the birth of my first child and my desire to re-tell the Christmas story was surely connected with becoming a father for the first time.

2018 saw the hottest summer on record for some time in Glasgow. My wife, Rachel, and I were expecting our first baby, which was due any day. It had been a difficult pregnancy in some ways. A scan, just before Christmas 2017, revealed a problem with the baby's right arm, which might have indicated something more serious and potentially life-threatening. We refused tests that would have offered no solution but carried a risk of abortion and, instead, prayed intensely, invoking the intercession of Venerable Margaret Sinclair – a blood relative of Rachel – that our next scan might have better results. As we erected the beautiful Nativity Set that was a wedding gift from my brother, we also began to pack up our belongings because circumstances meant that we found ourselves looking for a new house – a place to settle down and have our baby. Gazing upon that scene of the young couple with their tiny baby, I found myself looking towards Saint Joseph for strength and courage. He has never disappointed me.

That July, our son John-Paul Joseph entered the world. He was a bright, healthy baby with an upper limb difference in his right arm. Every day, we thank God for him. With every gurgle, every cry and every dirty nappy, he challenges us to live our vocation as Mary and Joseph did, offering the sacrifice of time and energy in love. His very life and, indeed, our choice to try to live the Gospel by getting married and starting a family is, in the words of holy Simeon, "a sign of contradiction". There has never been such an assault upon marriage and the family as there is today.

After the birth of Jesus in Bethlehem, and the subsequent flight into Egypt to avoid the mass infanticide ordered by the tyrant, Herod, Mary and Joseph present the Christ-child in the Temple. This is to fulfil the Law of Moses that every first-born should be presented to the Lord. Mary and Joseph undertake the religious education of God's Son in the way of their people. It is a challenge for every parent, especially amidst scandals in the Church committed against children.

In this climate, we all need to remind ourselves that Jesus is at the centre of what we believe. He remains a "Sign of Contradiction" to this day. I hope that this play surprises people and inspires them with the true hope of Christmas, which pully busy shepherds from their day-to-day work, intrigues wise men from afar to take a step closer, and enrages tyrants to this very day.

CAST OF CHARACTERS

Tom: *A homeless man. A mute.*
Joe: *An elderly homeless man.*
Mary: *A homeless woman.*
Josh: *A homeless man.*
Joseph: *A carpenter from Nazareth.*
Mary: *A young woman, betrothed to Joseph.*
Hapheth: A shepherd.
Shem: *A shepherd*
Miriam: *A worker in the Inn at Bethlehem*
Rebekha: *A worker in the Inn at Bethlehem.*
Naomi: *The wife of the Innkeeper at Bethlehem.*
Ruben: *The Innkeeper at Bethlehem.*
Sarah: *A servant in King Herod's palace*
Esther: *A servant in King Herod's palace*
Ruth: *Mary Friel*
Mendel: *A soldier in King Herod's guard.*
Shimon: *A soldier in King Herod's guard.*
Simeon: *An elderly holy man.*
Anna: *An elderly holy woman*
Laban: *A temple priest.*
Church Worker 1: *A volunteer in the local church.*
Church Worker 2: *A volunteer in the local church.*

Sign of Contradiction: The Christmas Story was originally performed by AGAP, the Archdiocese of Glasgow Arts Project, on tour during Advent 2018. The first performance took place in Saint Bartholomew's Parish, Castlemilk, Glasgow on 10th December 2018. The cast and crew were as follows:

Tom	*Joe McGuire*
Joe	*Hugh Welsh*
Mary	*Bernadette McCluskey*
Josh	*Eugene Robb*
Joseph/Shimon	*Russell Wheeler*
Mary	*Mekha Sabu*
Hapheth	*Thomas Shaw*
Shem/Mission Worker 2	*Tony Porter*
Miriam	*Angela Evans*
Rebekha	*Teresa Bentley*
Naomi/Ruth	*Mary Friel*
Ruben	*Joe McDonald*
Sarah	*Jean Byrne*
Esther/Mission Worker 1	*Janette Maley*
Mendel	*Iain Marshall*
Simeon	*Matthew Lynch*
Anna	*Mary Bailey*
Laban	*Tony Waterston*

Director/Writer	*Stephen Callaghan*
Technical Director/Sound	*Ronan O'Neill*
Lighting Design	*Zachary O'Neill*
Stage Manager	*Kathleen Dooley*
Live Music Performed by	*Joe McGuire*

A NOTE ON STAGING

The action of the play takes place across a split stage, with present-day characters off to the side and historical/Biblical scenes played out on the main area. Lighting might help to focus the attention of the audience on either section. The character of JOSH acts as a narrator, linking the action of the Biblical scenes with the present day. The present-day characters remain on stage throughout, with the Biblical characters performing in another area of the stage. Traditional carols played onstage softly by the character of TOM can also provide atmosphere and act as a linking device to between scenes.

PROLOGUE

The scene is set outdoors at night. On stage is a metal bin, inside which a fire is burning. Litter is scattered around. There is a couple of wooden crates nearby. On one of them, sits a homeless man in ragged clothes, wearing a woolen hat. He is huddled in his coat, hugging himself against the cold, his head slumped forward, dozing. His name is JOE. Near him, sits another man in similar clothes, softly playing an accordion. His name is TOM.

ENTER MARY. She is also homeless, wearing a heavy coat and wrapped up in a scarf and hat to keep warm. She holds in her hands a crumpled chip paper from which she is eating.

MARY: Joe! Joe, wake up!

JOE: Whit is it, Mary? Yir disturbin' ma kip.

MARY: Huv ah no telt ye tae be careful. Go tae sleep an' ye might die fae hypothermia. Whit've ye done wi' that newspaper ah gied ye?

JOE: Ah stuffed some o' it doon ma boots an' the rest, ah pit in the fire tae keep it gaun. (*Noticing the chips in her hands:*) Here, whit's that ye've goat there?

MARY: Fish supper.

JOE: Where did ye get that?

MARY: Aff some do-gooder that wis passin'. He'd had enough and gie'd the rest tae me. Want some?

JOE: Is it still warm?

MARY: Who are you, Gordon Ramsay? It's food, in't it?

JOE: Aye, gie's some chips. (*She goes over to JOE and he begins eating.*) Huv ye goat some for Tom?

MARY: He didnae ask.

JOE: He cannae talk, Mary. Whit's he gonnae say? (*To TOM:*) Tom, ye want some chips? They're aw cauld an' greasy but we're no Gordon Ramsay.

TOM stops playing and takes some chips.

MARY: He might no be able tae talk but if it wisnae for his playin, we wid be a lot worse off than we are now. At least he gets a few coppers in his bunnit[1] fur a tune. God love him!

JOE: Here, wur fire's gettin' awfie low. Have ye goat ony mare newspaper, Mary?

MARY: Naw, but there's a book shop doon the road that's closed doon an' they've dumped a few bags o' books ootside, waitin' oan the clenny[2] tae come.

JOE: Ah'm no wantin' tae read, ah'm wantin' tae keep warm.

MARY: Books burn jist as guid as newspapers if ye tear them up. Ah lifted a couple o' thick wans on the way by. Here...

---

[1] Bunnit – a bonnet (hat), commonly a flat cap

[2] Clenny – "Cleansing Department" (local authority department responsible for waste removal)

4

MARY produces a couple of books from her coat pockets or from a bag that she has over her arm. She hands them to JOE.

JOE: These are heavy books, Mary. Whit are they?

MARY: Ah don't care; the Daily Record burns as well as the Financial Times.

JOE: (*Looking at the first Book*) "Gone With the Wind" by Margaret Mitchell. That's a good yin.

MARY: Frankly my dear, I don't give a damn. Jist tear the pages oot an' shove them oan the fire.

JOE: It'll be the burnin' of Atlanta all over again. Whit's the other wan' ye've picked up? Some amount of pages in it. (*He looks inside the cover:*) Wait a minute, Mary. Ye cannae burn this.

MARY: Whit is it, Joe. Gie it tae me an' ah'll burn it fur ye.

JOE: No, Mary, ye cannae burn this wan. It's the Bible.

MARY: Are you tryin' tae be funny, Joe. We're blinkin' freezin' oot here an' you're worrying about burnin' an auld book?

JOE: This isnae just any book, Mary. It's the Bible. It's God's Word.

MARY: Well, ah'm no carin'. Unless Jesus turns up here an' magics up some heat fur us, ah'll be burnin' it.

Mary reaches for the Bible in Joe's hands but he pulls it away from her.

JOE: No, Mary. You go burnin' Bibles an' ye'll have plenty of heat where you're gaun.

MARY: Whit are you gonnae do wi' it?

JOE: Well, it's Christmas. Maybe we could read some o' it. Come on, Mary, when was the last time you heard the Christmas story?

MARY: Ach, Joe, you're gettin' sentimental in your auld age. Are you actually gonnae read the Bible oot?

JOE: Well, ah've no got the money tae go tae the pictures, have you?

> *Another figure approaches, he is also wrapped up against the cold.*

> *His name is JOSH.*

JOSH: Excuse me, would you mind if I joined you for some company and to share the heat of your fire?

MARY: Suit yersel' but ye'll need tae be quick – ma friend's just found religion an' he's readin' the fuel.

JOE: Sorry, pal, ah didnae catch yer name.

JOSH: You can call me Josh, if you like. I get called lots of names.

JOE: Don't we all.

MARY: Ah'm Mary, that's Tom – he cannae talk but he'll play ye a tune – and the Pope sittin' there is my pal, Joe.

JOSH: Joe – short for Joseph, I suppose.

JOE: Only, my mammy called me Joseph. (*JOSH chuckles.*) Whit's funny? Ah, bet your mammy never called ye "Josh" did she?

JOSH: No, I'm not laughing at that. I'm laughing at the fact that of all the people I could've met in the park on Christmas night, ah bump into Mary and Joseph.

MARY: (*Laughs*) Aye, well there's nae wean in a manger here.

JOE: Maybe Tom can be wan o' the animals in the stable...wis there no an ox or somethin'?

MARY: Well, at least we don't have to look far for an ass.

JOSH: I think Tom might be a wise man. Tom, do you know any Christmas carols? Maybe you could play something for us?

JOE: Actually, Josh, Mary just fun an auld Bible an' we were gonnae read the Christmas story.

JOSH: Aye, I'd be up for that.

MARY: Ah'm no listenin' to you readin' a bunch o' auld fairy tales that probably never happened.

JOSH: Why'd you say that, Mary?

MARY: Well, is there no somethin' aboot a Virgin gie'in birth an aw that? How's anybody meant tae believe that?

JOSH: Oh, you're talking about the prophesy of Isaiah?[3]

MARY: The whit?

JOE: Listen tae him, Mary, ye might learn somethin'.

---

[3] Isaiah 7:14

JOSH: Well, in the year 733 BC, there was a
prophesy. Just like today, people were fighting
with one another. There were four kings.

MARY: Wait a minute, I thought it was three kings
that went tae see the baby?

JOSH: No, this is over 700 years before that baby
was born. There were four kingdoms, three of
which were threatened by their powerful
neighbour, Assyria. King Ahaz of Judah feared
the power of the Assyrian King and pledged his
allegiance to him in exchange for protection
against his enemies, the Kings of Syria and Israel.
However, this allegiance came at a terrible price.
The Assyrian King demanded that Ahaz abandon
the true God and worship the pagan Gods of his
land. Ahaz bent to the will of the Assyrian King
and had an altar erected to the pagan gods of
Assyria in the Temple at Jerusalem. At that time,
there was a prophet called Isaiah, who went to
King Ahaz and chided him for his lack of faith in
the Lord and his reliance on human power. He

told him to ask the Lord for a sign, but King Ahaz was a shrewd politician and he said: "I will not put the Lord to the test."[4] So Isaiah told him: "The Lord Himself will give you a sign, and it is this: Behold – a Virgin shall conceive and bear a son, and shall call his name Emmanuel, which means 'God is with us'."[5]

JOE: So, you mean to tell us that over seven hundred years before the birth of Jesus, there was a prophecy that foretold His birth by the Virgin Mary?

JOSH: That's right.

JOE: That's incredible!

MARY: How dae you know aw this? This is better than the History Channel.

JOSH: Aye, there's more to the story than most people realise. At the time when Jesus is born, the

---

[4] Isaiah 7:12

[5] Isaiah 7:14

Roman Empire was the dominant world power. The Emperor Cesar had given himself the title "Augustus" which means "Saviour" and he set out to make himself the ruler of the known world. A Census was called, asking everyone to return to the place of his origin to report to the Roman Officials.

END OF PROLOGUE

SCENE ONE: MARY AND JOSEPH

ENTER JOSEPH, a young carpenter. He is sweeping the floor of his workshop.

ENTER MARY, his young wife.

MARY: God be with, Joseph.

JOSEPH: Mary! You've returned. I've missed you! How are you?

MARY: I am well.

JOSEPH: And the baby?

MARY: The baby thrives.

JOSEPH: And your cousin, Elizabeth?

MARY: She's absolutely radiant!

JOSEPH: And her child?

MARY: He is strong and healthy.

JOSEPH: A boy? That should please Zechariah. Do they have a name?

MARY: That is the strangest part of all. We are not the only ones to be given a name from God, Joseph.

JOSEPH: What do you mean?

MARY: It was Zechariah that received the word from God's messenger whilst he was in the temple, exercising his priestly ministry, that his wife would conceive. There was a flicker of doubt in his heart because Elizabeth has always been considered barren and this has brought her so much pain.

JOSEPH: Small-minded people see the childless womb as a curse.

MARY: Zechariah was told that the child's name would be John and from that moment on, he was struck dumb.

JOSEPH: Struck dumb?

MARY: Yes, not a word could he speak until after the birth, when they went to present the child in the temple and the priest asked for the child's name. Zechariah wrote on a tablet: "His name is John" and from that moment on, his speech was restored!

JOSEPH: Incredible and...frightening. I'm glad to hear that I was not the only one who doubted. I'm sorry, Mary. I should have believed you when you told me your news.

MARY: You needed God to reveal it to you. You are an honourable man, Joseph. You could have broken our betrothal and dismissed me.

JOSEPH: And you would have died. An unmarried woman, betrothed to a man and found to be with child to another - the people of Nazareth would have stoned you to death. Even if I had broken our bond, I would have done it privately and spared you that.

MARY: I know but, you will take me as your wife and we will raise this child for God. I'm sure I felt him leap for joy in my womb when I went to see Elizabeth.

JOSEPH: Mary, I have some news for you. I was talking to a customer this morning and he told me that the Roman Governor has ordered a census to take place throughout the land.

MARY: When?

JOSEPH: Some time soon. Six months, he said. He may be wrong.

MARY: What does it mean for us?

JOSEPH: Each person is to return to the land of his ancestors. My family is of the house and line of David. We must travel to Bethlehem, the land of my forefathers. It will be a long journey. Ninety miles and it will be tough. I have bought a new beast to take us there. Gad sold him to me. A fine specimen of a donkey. He will carry you and the child.

MARY: (*Smiles*) Ah, so that's how it happens.

JOSEPH: What do you mean? How what happens?

MARY: Scripture says that the Messiah is to be born in Bethlehem.[6]

> *The lights fade to black.*

> *The action returns to the park where JOSH continues the story with the other characters listening.*

JOSH: So, Mary and Joseph travelled to the land of Joseph's ancestors. The city of the great King of Israel, David. It had been foretold that there would come a Mighty God, a Wonderful Counsellor, a Prince of Peace who sit upon the throne of King David and his reign would last forever![7] But God chose to reveal this great event in some of the most unlikely places.

END OF SCENE ONE

---

[6] Micah 5:1-5

[7] Cf. Isaiah 9:6

SCENE TWO: THE SHEPHERDS

There is the sound of sheep bleating.

Two Shepherds, SHEM and HAPHETH sit,
huddled up against the cold.

SHEM: Cauld night, eh?

HAPHETH: Aye.

SHEM: Feel it in ma bones.

HAPHETH: Aye.

SHEM: Wish I'd brought another jaikit[8].

HAPHETH: Whit are you wantin'? A cuddle? Well,
    yer ontae plums – jump up an doon or stamp yer
    feet and ye'll soon warm up.

SHEM: See when yer oot in the fields, it gies ye an
    eerie feelin', doesn't it?

HAPHETH: Whit dae ye mean?

---

[8] Jacket

SHEM: Ah mean, you've been dae'in this a lot longer than me but, when yer oot in the fields at night, does it no gie ye the willies[9]?

HAPHETH: Only thing that gies me the willies is seein' ma sheep gettin' attacked by a wolf so keep yer eyes peeled.

There is a brief pause as SHEM looks up at the night sky.

SHEM: Vast isn't it? Absolutely vast.

HAPHETH: Whit are you on aboot, Shem?

SHEM: The sky. Just look at the stars. Makes you think about it all, doesn't it?

HAPHETH: You're no huvin' them deep thoughts again, ur ye?

SHEM: "Ah'll make yer descendents as many as the stars in the heavens."[10] That's what the Lord said to Abraham, remember?

---

[9] "Gies ye the willies" – gives you an eerie feeling

HAPHETH: Aye, ah remember.

SHEM: That's us, you know. We're his descendents. The people of Israel. The people of Abraham, Isaac and Jacob's God. A people as many as the stars in the heavens. Just like he promised.

HAPHETH: Aye, well, He's made a lot mair promises that ah'm still waitin' tae see fulfilled.

SHEM: What do you mean?

HAPHETH: Well, what about this Messiah person that's meant to come and restore Israel. Where's Israel now, eh? Whit happened King David's dynasty that wis supposed tae last forever? Whit happened tae that promise tae David? "A son, the fruit of yer loins will sit oan yer throne and his reign will last forever."[11] Did God just forget aboot that wan?

SHEM: Maybe there's more to it.

---

[10] Cf. Genesis 22:17

[11] Psalm 132:11

HAPHETH: How can you say that? Israel's in the grubber! David's line's died oot. How's God gonnae restore Israel when the Roman Empire's occupyin' the land and taxin' the hell oot o' the people, eh? Whit kind o' king have we got noo?

SHEM: Hapheth, I know what you think of King Herod – ah've had tae listen tae ye grumblin' aboot him every time I'm oot here working wi' ye.

HAPHETH: Herod the Great! The great whit? Great tyrant! Building aw they fancy buildings an' taxin' ordinary folk tae pay for them. Panderin' tae Rome like a blinkin' brown-nosed lapdog! Dae you know that he had a statue of a golden eagle put up ootside the temple in Jerusalem? Never mind the fact that it's a graven image, it's a blinkin' monument tae oor oppressors! Roman swine!

SHEM: Good job he cannae hear ye oot here, Hapheth. Herod wouldnae think twice about torchin' your hoose and murderin' yer wife an' weans[12]. They say he's got spies everywhere in the cities and towns listening oot for treasonous remarks.

HAPHETH: He's out of his mind. Besides, we're away out in the fields. Nearest town is Bethlehem.

SHEM: Anyway, how do you know about that eagle outside the temple? You cannae go into the temple any mair than ah can. We're ritually unclean.

HAPHETH: That's because we work wi' the sheep. We tend the sheep day and night, smell yer clothes and they smell of their...

SHEM: Aw right. Well, we might no be able tae go intae the temple but ah still pray. Dae you pray, Hapheth?

HAPHETH: Depends whit ye mean by prayin'.

---

[12] "Weans" - children

SHEM: Ah remember bits fae the Torah and if a wee bit o' scripture goes through ma heid, ah take that as a sign fae the Lord.

HAPHETH: Whit puts me aff is aw the hypocrisy that goes oan wi the priests and scribes. Big hooses and fancy claes[13], tellin' people whit tae dae but no daein' it themselves.

SHEM: Aye, there's a lot o' that but ah wouldnae let that take ma faith away fae me. My faith means too much for the actions o' men tae rob me o' it. D'ye no remember the Psalm that says: "It is better to take refuge in the Lord than to trust in Man"[14]?

HAPHETH: Aye, an' ah remember what the Prophet Jeremiah said: "Cursed is the man who trusts in mankind, who makes the flesh his strength and turns his heart from the Lord"[15]. Ah've nae faith in men.

---

[13] "Big hooses and fancy claes": Big houses and fancy clothes.

[14] Psalm 118:9

SHEM: But the Lord has faith in us. Ah believe that. Ah teach ma children that. Ah want them tae be able tae worship in the Temple and honour Israel's God in peace. God established the priesthood through Moses and Aaron an' an' ah'll no mock it.

HAPHETH: Well, suit yersel'. Ma wife's the same. She still prays a fair bit. Honours the Lord for every bit of food that passes through the weans mouths and intae their bellies. That's true faith...no scrubbin' pots and aw that stuff that they dae in the temple. Noo, enough o' this holy talk – are we havin' a swally[16] the night or whit? Where's yer bottle?

SHEM: Hapheth...

HAPHETH: Oh, whit is it noo?

SHEM: You're still angry, aren't ye?

---

[15] Jeremiah 17:5

[16] "Swally" – a drink

HAPHETH: Aye...aye, ah suppose ah am. You
would be too, if your son was born blind. You
know what they say, don't you? They say it's a
sign of a curse. They say it's God's anger visited
upon him because of some sin committed by a
past generation. (*Breaking down:*) Well, what
happened tae the promised Messiah that wis
supposed tae come and make the deaf hear an' the
blind see?[17] Where is he noo?

> *Shem goes over to Hapheth and puts an
> arm around him as he weeps. He hands
> him a bottle from his pocket.*

SHEM: The Lord hasn't forgotten his promise,
Hapheth. To God, a thousand years is like a day.
We don't know when He will send us a Saviour,
but He will. I believe it. There are still
descendants of King David. They might not be
royalty any more but remember that David was a
shepherd like you and me when God called
him...and you know what the Prophet Micah says:

---

[17] Isaiah 35:5

"But you, O Bethlehem Ephrathah, who are the least among the clans of Judah, from you shall come forth for me one who is to be ruler in Israel, whose coming forth is from of old, from ancient days."[18]

HAPHETH: He will come from Bethlehem...

SHEM: Wait...do you hear that?

HAPHETH: Oh, Shem, ah'm no in the mood! Wait, ah hear it too!

SHEM: Sounds like singing...but nicer than singing...

> *Suddenly, a bright light shines upon them and they look up, startled. They fall on their knees and cover their faces. A loud clear voice is heard...*

VOICE: Do not be afraid. I bring news of great joy!

> *The Shepherds freeze and the light fades to black.*

---

[18] Micah 5:2

The action returns to the park where JOSH continues the story with the other characters listening.

JOSH: So, you see, the first people that God invited to meet his Son were those that didn't feel welcome in the places of worship. The ritually unclean. The Angel of the Lord told them to go to Bethlehem where they would find a baby wrapped in swaddling clothes and lying in a manger.

END OF SCENE TWO

SCENE THREE: THE INN

Centre-stage is a table, which acts as a stove and work surface. There is a basin on the table at one side and a large pot at the other side with a ladle in it. MIRIAM stands stirring the pot. She adds a pinch of something, stirs it again and tastes the contents from the ladle. As she does this, REBEKHA enters carrying a stack of plates and cups, which she takes to the basin.

REBEKHA: It's absolutely hoachin'[19] in there! Punters from everywhere.

MIRIAM: It's that ruddy Census that's done it, you know. Apparently, the Roman Emperor has ordered a census to take place and everybody has to go to the land of their origin to be registered.

REBEKHA: Well, Miriam, all I can say is that there must be a heck of a lot of people who come from Bethlehem.

MIRIAM: Wasn't King David from Bethlehem?

[19] "Absolutely hoachin'" – Very busy.

REBEKHA: Aye, I think so but if he's in there, I
    didn't recognise him for aw his descendents who
    are in there fillin' their faces an' getting merry on
    the wine.

ENTER NAOMI, the wife of the Innkeeper.

NAOMI: That's six more plates of stew, Miriam.
    Have we got enough lamb?

MIRIAM: Yes, I think so, Ma'am.

NAOMI: Good, we'll need it, and bake some more
    bread. I've never seen the place so busy!

REBEKHA: Lord bless the Emperor Cesar Augustus,
    eh?

NAOMI: Watch your tongue, Rebekha. I won't have
    you blaspheme in this house! Although, I must
    say that Cesar has been good to us with this silly
    census he's having. I wouldn't grudge him a
    small blessing these days. It's good for business.

REBEKHA: Yes, ma'am.

MIRIAM: Keeps us in our jobs too.

NAOMI: When you're done with the cooking, Miriam, there are a couple of people waiting to get into their rooms. We just sold the last two. Make sure they have fresh towels and that the hearth is swept.

MIRIAM: You mean the rooms are all full?

NAOMI: Yes, and get that stew ready for those six people sitting by the window on the right.

MIRIAM: Yes, ma'am.

REBEKHA: It's a cold night out there. People must be glad to come in and find shelter.

NAOMI: Rebekha, when you're done with those dishes, take the slops out to the animals in the stable. Just dump them in the manger. Right, I must go and see to the customers.

   NAOMI exits.

REBEKHA: I can't believe that! "Take the slops out to the animals!" What does she think I am?

MIRIAM: A paid servant and if you don't stop complaining, you'll be out on your ear if Naomi catches you.

REBEKHA: Nah, I don't need to worry. Her man's got a soft spot for me.

MIRIAM: Oh, aye? You and everyone else. He's soft-hearted.

REBEKHA: Aye, and soft-headed for marrying Naomi. I feel sorry for him.

MIRIAM: Shush, here he's coming.

ENTER RUBEN, the Innkeeper.

RUBEN: Good evening, ladies. That stew smells delicious, Miriam. Mind if I have a taste?

MIRIAM: Not at all, Ruben. Shall I serve you up a bowl?

RUBEN: Have you seen Naomi? She was looking after a group of travellers who were sitting in the corner by the window. I think they just ordered some food.

REBEKHA walks over and smiles at him.

REBEKHA: Well, she did come in a short time ago. She asked me to take the slops out to the animals in the stable. I don't have to do that, do I, Ruben? (*She leans in close to him in a flirty fashion.*) I mean, you wouldn't want me to be smelling of animals, now would you? I'd have to wear extra perfume. Do you like my perfume, Ruben?

MIRIAM hands RUBEN a plate of stew.

RUBEN: My that smells very alluring indeed!

MIRIAM: Must be the herbs and onion, I used.

ENTER NAOMI, who marches up between REBEKHA and RUBEN.

NAOMI: (*Directed at Rebekha*) Yes, even if it is mutton dressed as lamb! (*Grabbing the plate out of*

Ruben's hand:) Right, five more plates of stew, when you're ready, Miriam! Customers are waiting! And, as for you, Rebekha; why don't you take those slops out to the animals? Perhaps the night air will cool your passions.

> *REBEKHA huffs and EXITS carrying a bucket of slops.*

RUBEN: Now, darling, she was only...

NAOMI: Come on, you! Customers need to be served. Get another three jugs of wine from the cellar and don't go helping yourself to it on the way up.

RUBEN: But darling, I only have a little bit to keep warm...

NAOMI: Enough! And don't forget to charge the customers extra if you top up their cups. We can't run this place on thin air! You're too soft, Ruben – you've always been too soft! Thought I was marrying a businessman and look at you! A sorry excuse for a publican! If my father were still alive, he would say....

Suddenly, there's a shriek and REBEKHA enters in a panic.

MIRIAM: What is it, Rebekha?

REBEKHA: I took the slops into the stable, like you asked me, ma'am. It was dark but I had my lantern and when I got there, I could see another lantern was glowing inside. I could see the beasts huddled together beside the manger so I went forward with the bucket of slops and then, when I went to empty it in the manger, I saw a figure stirring in the corner. It was a man! He called out and stopped me, just in time. Then I saw it!

NAOMI: Saw what, girl?

MIRIAM: Did the man hurt you?

REBEKHA: No. I looked down and there was a baby in the manger! A tiny little baby! I got such

34

a fright that I screamed and then I felt a hand on my wrist.

MIRIAM: The man? Was it the man? Did he grab you?

REBEKHA: No, it was a woman. A young woman who was curled up in the straw beside the manger. Her arm was hung over the top, caressing the baby's head. She was beside the donkey. It was like it was keeping her warm.

NAOMI: Right, well, I'll soon put an end to this! Young vagabonds think they can just trespass on our property and get away with it. I'll soon show them.

RUBEN: Wait. Um...Naomi, I can explain this.

NAOMI: What are you talking about, Ruben? There's a baby in the animals' food trough!

RUBEN: I know. I suggested it. In fact, I was just about to offer them a plate of Miriam's lovely lamb stew when you took it away from me.

NAOMI: You knew about this, Ruben? You knew that there was a young couple with a baby in our stable?

RUBEN: Yes, I offered it to them. It was all we had. The girl is called Mary and the man is called, Joseph. They came all the way from Nazareth and they were desperate. She was so close to her time and you had just rented out the last room that we had upstairs.

NAOMI: From Nazareth? Well, that's typical. Probably come from Galilee. Scum of the earth.

RUBEN: They were very nice, Naomi. I had to offer them something. All of the inns were full. It's the census, you see.

NAOMI: I know it's the census, you idiot! We've never been so busy!

RUBEN: Then, surely, we can afford to help a young couple who have nowhere to stay? It's the least we can do.

NAOMI: (*Pauses to draw breath*) Alright, Ruben. Have it your way. But you charge them for that stew!

RUBEN: I will not! Just remember that it's my name that's above that door, Naomi, and I shall do as I please. That young couple can stay in that stable for as long as they like.

NAOMI: Right, well, in that case, I'll go and see to that party of Pharisees that just walked in. Let's hope they tip well. At least one of us is trying to make some money tonight!

NAOMI exits in a strop.

RUBEN: Miriam, please be kind enough to take two plates of warm stew to the young couple out in the stable.

MIRIAM: Certainly, Ruben.

RUBEN: And, Rebekha, perhaps you could take them out some blankets and towels and a basin of hot water for them to wash.

REBEKHA: Alright. (*Looking offstage.*) But, Ruben, it
looks like they might have some visitors arriving.
Some shepherds just came up to the stable door.
It looks as if they are kneeling down in front of the
manger.

RUBEN: Be careful not to draw attention. This
young couple are to be left in peace. Perhaps you
might also take some stew to their visitors also.

> *The lights fade to black.*

> *The action returns to JOSH sitting by the fire
> with the other characters in the opening scene.*

JOSH: The shepherds must have been astonished to
find the promised Saviour of the World lying in
an animals' feeding trough at the back of a pub.
It's hard to imagine anything further from the
regal majesty of the Roman Emperor Cesar
Augustus who was declaring himself to be the
"Saviour of the World and Prince of Peace".
Nevertheless, there were others who recognised
that a great world event was about to take place

and those that study the stars could see that the alignment of the planets suggested that a great king was about to be born...but in Jerusalem, the puppet King of the Roman Empire, Herod the Great was less than pleased.

END OF SCENE THREE

SCENE FOUR: COURT OF KING HEROD

Three women enter. They are servants in the court of King Herod. There is an air of urgency and even of secrecy.

SARAH: Listen to me, we must ensure that everything is ready for the soldiers when they return. Esther?

ESTHER: Yes, Sarah?

SARAH: Make sure that there are salts to pour into the water when they are bathing and fragrant oils to anoint them. They will need it to forget what they have been through. And, Ruth?

RUTH: Yes, my lady?

SARAH: You are to ensure that there is a good supply of wine. It will deaden the memory of their deeds and encourage sleep.

ESTHER: But, my lady – will you tell us what is going on?

SARAH: Sit down, both of you. Make sure the door is locked. I don't want this conversation to be overheard. Herod has spies in every corner.

Ruth checks the door and the three women sit down.

You two have been like sisters to me since we began in the King's service. I have kept your confidences. Will you keep mine?

RUTH: Of course. When Fishel couldn't keep his hands off me and I felt afraid, it was you that I spoke to, Sarah.

ESTHER: And I trusted you when I found out that my father was planning to divorce my mother.

SARAH: Yes, and so I will trust you. A number of soldiers were sent to the land of Judah, to the town of Bethlehem to carry out a terrible action. I heard Herod give the order myself. You remember those strange men who arrived from the East to seek an audience with King Herod?

ESTHER: I saw them arriving at the gates. I'd never seen such a thing. They arrived on camels laden with all kinds of strange things.

SARAH: That's them. I think they came from Persia but I couldn't be sure.

RUTH: I saw them too. Such strange exotic clothes!

SARAH: They must have caught Herod's eye because he allowed them in. One of them was carrying something like a leather tube, presumably containing some scrolls of parchment. All three of them had grave expressions.

ESTHER: I thought that one of them was an old man. He had a long white beard and his hair was hidden under a turban. He had the most penetrating eyes. Like his youth had left him prematurely and left him only with serious thoughts and heavy business.

RUTH: One of them had skin the colour of coal. I've never seen a man like that. He was beautiful, graceful. He moved like some great exotic bird.

Like he glided along the floor in his robes, rather than walked.

ESTHER: I know! And the other one was much younger. He didn't have a beard but his skin was ruddy, like he had done a lot of travelling. He had that same serious expression though. He smelled amazing. Like the pores of his skin were steeped in spices.

RUTH: Seems like he caught your eye, anyway, Esther!

SARAH: Listen to me. I oversaw the servants during the meal. Herod was his usual self, trying to suss out their motives but I could see that he was intrigued by the three foreigners because of their wealth and splendour. As usual, he had his manservant taste his wine three times in case there was any attempt to poison him.

RUTH: Hah! We should be so lucky!

SARAH: Then, one of the visitors – the one with the white beard – said "We seek the King of the

Jews". Herod's brows knitted at first and I
thought he might be about to get angry but then
he reclined and said: "Congratulations! You've
found him."

ESTHER: What a peacock!

SARAH: Then the old man unfurled the leather tube
and a parchment opened out.

RUTH: What was it?

SARAH: Some kind of map of the stars. It was very
impressive. Herod leaned in and looked at it with
great intent. It seems that these three travellers
had followed the course of the stars in search of
the One promised to our people.

RUTH: The Messiah? Are you serious?

SARAH: Yes, apparently so. They had studied the
stars and believed that their findings had led them
in the direction of Bethlehem in the land of Judah
to where a child would be born and that child
would be the new King of Israel.

ESTHER: Are the prophesies actually about to be fulfilled? Isaiah said: "Caravans of camels shall fill you, dromedaries from Midian and Ephah; all from Sheba shall come bearing gold and frankincense, and proclaiming the praises of the Lord".[20]

RUTH: It certainly sounds familiar.

SARAH: I could see that Herod was unsettled by the news and immediately asked them to find out the exact location of the infant King and bring him news of his whereabouts so that he too might pay him homage. After that, the visitors seemed keen to leave. Herod tried to get them to stay but they made their apologies and left as soon as they could.

RUTH: I'm not surprised. Herod has a habit of wiping out the people who get in his way. He banished his first wife and child and we all know that he's executed members of the Sanhedrin.

---

[20] Isaiah 60:6

SARAH: But the order he gave this time was even worse. Every child in Bethlehem, under the age of two, is to be hunted down and killed.

ESTHER: That's terrible!

Suddenly two soldiers enter, SHIMON and MENDEL. They are soiled with blood and sweat. SHIMON is traumatised.

MENDEL: Sarah, get a basin, some hot water and smelling salts.

RUTH: I'll do it.

Ruth goes to fetch a basin.

SHIMON: I can't think about it. I just can't think about it, Mendel.

MENDEL: Come now, man. You only did what you were ordered to do. You only did your duty.

SHIMON: What kind of excuse is that? I didn't sign up for murdering babies!

MENDEL: You are only carrying out Herod's orders.

SHIMON: God will judge us for this! His hand will smite us for this!

MENDEL: Control yourself, man! Hurry up with that basin.

> *Ruth arrives with the basin and puts it in front of Shimon.*

SHIMON: I...I can't....

> *He grabs the basin from her hands and vomits into it.*

MENDEL: Best bring him some wine. He won't last the night without it.

> *Ruth takes the basin away and Esther hands Mendel a flagon of wine, which he swigs from.*

MENDEL: Now, listen to me Shimon, you need to drink this wine and let it go straight to your head.

SHIMON: I still hear their cries, Mendel! The
mothers, clawing up my back as I went in there. I
have never taken the life of a child! Their cries
pierce my heart!

MENDEL: You did what you had to do. You don't
have to like it.

SHIMON: I had to kill a baby in the womb of its
mother. She went to stop me from killing her
other son and I had to...I had to kill the one inside
her... How can I live with myself?

Mendel is stunned.

SARAH: Shimon, you must pray to the Lord for
forgiveness. You must lay down in sackcloth and
ashes. You must plead for God's mercy.

SHIMON: Their blood cries out for vengeance from
the very ground![21]

*Mendel hits Shimon over the head with the hilt
of his sword and he passes out.*

---

[21] Cf. Genesis 4:10

SARAH: Why did you do that?

MENDEL: I had no choice. He was hysterical. Besides, he wouldn't want to be awake through what I've got to do next.

SARAH: What do you mean?

MENDEL: Herod has ordered the execution of one of his own sons. I'm the one who has to do the deed.

SARAH: Don't do it, I beg you! These are the actions of a lunatic, obsessed with power and afraid to lose it.

MENDEL: Exactly. I know that. And I also know that the person who kills Herod's son will most likely be executed next, so I ask you to keep Shimon out of it. He has a family. I don't. Comfort him, Sarah.

MENDEL exits.

The lights fade.

The action returns to JOSH sitting with the other characters as in the opening scene.

JOSH: The slaughter of the innocents was one of the cruellest acts that Herod would commit. He went down in history as one of the most vicious tyrants who ever lived. Anyone who was a threat to his power was killed, including several members of his own family. In fact, the Emperor Cesar Augustus is said to have remarked that it was safer to be Herod's pig than Herod's son because the Jews didn't slaughter pigs. But what became of Mary and Joseph and the baby? Well, Joseph was warned in a dream to take the child and his mother and escape into Egypt until Herod was dead. The wise men were wise enough not to go back to Herod with the news of the child's whereabouts. Some time later, Mary and Joseph were able to return home and begin a life in Nazareth. But first, the requirements of the Law of Moses had to be fulfilled.

END OF SCENE FOUR.

SCENE FIVE: THE TEMPLE

The stage is set with an altar table, on which sits a menorah with candles lit.

An old woman is praying by the side of the altar with her hands raised in supplication. She is ANNA, a woman who dedicates herself to service in the Temple.

ANNA: "I see him, though not now; I behold him, though not near: A star shall advance from Jacob and a staff shall rise from Israel…"[22]

Enter SIMEON. An old, holy man.

SIMEON: Ah, Anna, I recognise that text. It is from the Book of Numbers. Moses awaiting the promised Messiah who would come to redeem God's people. How I have longed to see that promise fulfilled in my own days.

---

[22] Numbers 24:17

ANNA: You shall, Simeon. The Lord has revealed this to you. You will not taste death until you have laid eyes upon the Anointed One of God.

SIMEON: Indeed, it was said to me that this would be so, but I am weary. I am reminded of the book of Lamentations, Anna: "Their skin has shrivelled on their bones; it has become as dry as a stick."[23] I am old.

ANNA: God gives life. Each one of us has his own allotted number of days. I feel that his time draws very near and "in His days, righteousness will flourish and peace until the moon fails."[24]

>   *ENTER Laban, a priest in the temple, carrying a small box or cage.*

SIMEON: Laban, are you looking for us?

LABAN: No, Simeon. I am about to conduct the ritual of cleansing and circumcision, prescribed by

---

[23] Lamentations 4:8

[24] Psalm 72:7

the Law of Moses. A young couple is waiting outside with their child. I am carrying the two turtle doves that they brought as an offering.

ANNA: "Two turtle doves or two young pigeons"[25].. ..the offering of the poor, Simeon. Could this be he that was promised?

SIMEON: Who are the parents, please Laban?

LABAN: The boy's father is Joseph of the House of David and his mother is called Mary and her people are from Nazareth.

SIMEON: What name do they give the child?

LABAN: The child is to be called Jesus.

ANNA: The name which means "One who Saves".

SIMEON: At last a Saviour is born to us – he is Christ the Lord.

ANNA: We long to see him, Laban. Please make haste.

[25] Leviticus 12:8

LABAN exits.

SIMEON: Can it be that God's promise is at last
  fulfilled?

ANNA: Let us praise the Lord.

> *ENTER LABAN followed by MARY and
> JOSEPH. Mary is holding the Child Jesus,
> wrapped in swaddling clothes.*

JOSEPH: We come to consecrate our first-born son to
  the Lord, as prescribed in the Law of Moses.

> *SIMEON approaches the child, awestruck.*

SIMEON: May I hold him, please?

> *Mary hands the child to Simeon who smiles at
> him.*

SIMEON: Look, Anna – it is indeed true! At last, all
  powerful Master, you allow your servant to go in
  peace as you have promised; for my eyes have
  seen your salvation, which you have made known

to the nations; a light to enlighten the gentiles and give glory to your people, Israel!

JOSEPH: You are indeed a holy man and we would be pleased to have your blessing. I am Joseph of the House of David and this is my wife, Mary.

SIMEON looks at Mary.

SIMEON: Look, he is destined for the fall and for the rise of many in Israel, destined to be a sign of contradiction and a sword will pierce your own soul too, so that the secret thoughts of many will be revealed.

Mary takes the baby in her arms again and bows to Simeon.

ANNA: My dear child, I was married only seven years when my husband passed away. Since then, I have dedicated my life to serving the Lord. We must praise God for what he calls each of us to do; in sorrow and in joy.

MARY: My soul glorifies the Lord. My spirit rejoices in God, my Saviour. He has looked upon his handmaid in her lowliness and from this day forward all generations will call me blessed. The Almighty works marvels for me! Holy is His name! He has put forth his mighty arm and scattered the proud-hearted! He casts the mighty from their thrones and raises up the lowly. To the starving he gives good things and sends the rich away empty. He protects Israel, his servant, remembering his mercy promised to Abraham and his offspring in every generation.

The lights fade to black.

END OF SCENE FIVE

EPILOGUE

The action returns to the group of homeless
people by the fire in the park.

MARY: And that was the end of it?

JOSH: No, that was really just the beginning. Joseph
and Mary took the child Jesus to their home in
Nazareth in Galilee, where he grew to manhood
and learned Joseph's trade as a carpenter. Then,
thirty years later, he started to preach the Good
News that the Kingdom of God was among us.

JOE: And then they killed him, didn't they?

JOSH: Aye, but the story didn't end there and that's
a story for another time. (handing the Bible to
Mary) Oh, sorry – here's your Bible. I don't know
what you want to do with it.

MARY: Ah think ah'll just hang onto it fur a wee
while. We burnt "Gone With the Wind" instead.

JOE: Well, thanks fur sharin' the story wi' us, Josh. Ah've never thought aboot it like that. The Saviour of the World started off homeless, just like us.

JOSH: Aye, and he remained close to the poor always.

JOE: Happy Christmas, Josh.

MARY: Oh, aye, ah forgot. Happy Christmas. Ah've nae mistletoe.

JOE: Just as well.

JOSH: Happy Christmas.

MARY: Well, we've nae turkey and nae bevvy[26] but we can maybe still have a few carols to cheer us up, eh Tom.

JOSH: I hope you don't mind, but I brought some food. Would you mind if I break bread with you?

JOE: Of, course, Josh. Ah'm starvin'.

[26] "Bevvy" – alcoholic beverages

JOSH produces a loaf of bread, which he holds up.

Suddenly, there is a bright light surrounding him. He breaks the bread and hands it to JOE and MARY. They fall to their knees. The next thing, JOSH has vanished.

MARY: Where did he go? I felt like my heart was burning in my chest.

JOE: What the heck just happened there?

TOM stands up.

TOM: Ah, think that was Jesus.

JOE: Aye, well said.

Suddenly, they realise that TOM just spoke and they stare in awe.

ENTER TWO MISSION VOLUNTEERS.

MISSION VOLUNTEER 1: Hello there, you're looking cold. We're volunteers from the Church across the road.

MISSION VOLUNTEER 2: We have some blankets and a hot meal if you would like to come over to the hall and join us.

MISSION VOLUNTEER 1: Is that a Bible you've got there?

MARY: (*Open-mouthed*) Aye...it is.

MISSION VOLUNTEER 2: Well, in that case, you don't need any explanation for what we're doing.

MISSION VOLUNTEER 1: Merry Christmas.

The lights fade to black.

THE END

Printed in Great Britain
by Amazon

25625244R00040